Letters from an Expatriate in Europe

Rabindranath Tagore

§§

ISBN 978-93-5126-592-4
Translation Copyright © A. Datta.
Based on Rabindranath Tagore's work in Bengali in
the public domain.
Language: American English.
Revision: Jul 2013.

Translated and published by A. Datta
lookingglassscrolls@live.in

First Print: Jul 2013.
Printed by Createspace.com in the USA.
Printed by Pothi.com in India.

US Price: $9.00
https://createspace.com/4365677

Presentation:

I place this book on your two hands,
my older brother Jyoti,
to whom my thoughts turned most often during my stay in England.

Affectionately,

Rabi

Table of Contents

Prologue

My friends requested me to release these letters and I obliged but reluctantly since most of these were not written for the 'Bharati'. As a consequence, I hadn't been sufficiently cautious in expressing my opinions. My reactions to foreign society and culture have been spontaneous. Whatever good or ill effects may be derived from such spontaneous expression, it at least gives a brief history of how a Bengali visiting England forms and alters his views.

Methinks the Bengali language had been rightly chosen for writing these letters. Talking to one's kin in the native tongue and writing to them in another doesn't feel right.

The views of the esteemed editor of the Bharati expressed in response to these letters have also been compiled since views always have two sides and it is necessary for the reader to know both.

[Translator's Note: 'Letters from an Expatriate in Europe' has been published in multiple forms in the original Bengali. This translation excludes the assertions of the author's oldest brother Dwijendranath Tagore who edited the periodical, Bharati. They do not accompany the book in Rabindranath Tagore's complete works.]

My First Letter

We boarded the steamer 'Poona' on 20 September and she set sail at five o'clock as we thronged her roof to watch the last signs of the Indian coast gradually fade out of sight. I retired into my cabin oppressed by the din resulting from so many people talking at once. I see no good reason to hide from you that my mind was already in the doldrums, but away with that for I have neither the inclination nor the leisure to complain thus; and even if I did I wouldn't succeed in gaining your sympathies or would make you run out of patience.

At your feet O! mighty ocean for I alone know how I bore the passage of the six days that followed. You must already know what seasickness is, but I suppose not what it is like. I was visited by this malady and a detailed account of it would cause a rock to shed tears. Yes sir, for six days I hadn't left my bed. My cabin was small and dimly lit and all its windows were permanently shut lest sea-water intrude it. For six days I was barely alive—I had neither seen the face of the sun nor been touched by so much as a breeze. It was only on the first evening that a fellow passenger had forced me to get out of bed and had taken me to the dining table. As I took to my feet, the elements beneath my skull took to each others' throats and started a riot. I could neither see nor walk and was seized by an attack of vertigo. Having taken a couple of steps I sat down heavily on a bench. But the kind soul managed to get me out on the deck and I leaned on a rail. It was dark and the sky was overcast. We were sailing against the wind. Our ship progressed belching fire on two sides, through the pitch darkness of what appeared to be a harborless, shoreless ocean. Amidst the darkness the sea's surface swelled up again and again creating a sombre sight.

But I couldn't stand there for long. My lack of balance got the better of me and I had to be assisted back to my cabin on reaching which I lay down on my bed. In the six days that followed I hadn't once lifted my head. The steward was very kind to me. All day long he would maintain a supply of various edibles to my cabin and made sure that I ate something for according to him if I didn't eat I would grow as weak as a rat. He was quite willing to do anything for my betterment. For that I expressed my deep gratitude many times and before leaving ship I did following tradition convey to him something more material.

The sea grew much calmer as we neared Aden six days later. The steward kept encouraging me to leave bed and I finally obliged. But when I did I realized that my limbs had indeed grown as powerless as those of a little rat. There seemed to be a mismatch of sorts between my head and shoulders and my whole body felt like stolen garments that wouldn't fit. I left the cabin for its roof and there leaned on a chair. Out at last under the open sky! In the afternoon we spotted a small boat on the breast of the sea, but still no sign of land! This surprised us all. The folks on that boat began waving at us and our steamer was stopped. Out of them a small group of men got out in an even smaller boat and boarded our ship. All of them were Arabs and they were sailing from Aden to Muscat. They had lost their way, and all their drinking water when their barrels ruptured and their boat was carrying a modest number of sea-borne travelers. Our ship's crew gave them water and they were shown their bearings and distance from Muscat with the help of a map. But none of us were convinced that they would be able to make it to Muscat on their own.

I woke up on Saturday, 28 September at dawn to be greeted by a group of hills facing us. The morning was clear and beautiful, in fact it was just past sunrise and the sea was very calm. The hilly landscape in the distance was looking very beauteous at this hour. The colorful clouds seemed to be drooping on the hill-tops, weakened and drunk with endless sun-rays. And there were picturesque little sail-boats on the mirror-like sea.

Having reached Aden, I started writing a letter home but soon realized that the continuous motion to which I had been subject had created a kind of chaotic anarchy in the domain of my thoughts. I was daunted by the prospect of accomplishing the task. My thoughts seemed to resemble cobwebs that disintegrate when touched and I just couldn't decide what should follow what. Since I started writing in this condition there isn't much reason for you to regret that I never finished.

You see, I have developed some disrespect for the sea. What it is really like didn't quite live up to my notion of what it should be like. From the shores, the sea looks intimidating but not so from within and there is a reason for that. When I observed it from the shores of Bombay I had seen the blue offing melt into the blue skies in the horizon. In my imagination, I would fancy overcoming the drapes of the horizon to reveal the welling up of a shoreless, endless ocean. I would imagine what might lie there. It didn't seem straightforward that beyond this horizon there would be another. But in mid-ocean one's ship appears captive to the encircling horizon rather than being a moving vessel. This horizon is so limited in comparison to human imagination that it fails to impress. But you see, you must keep this a secret. All the greats right from Balmiki to Byron have been enraptured by the ocean. Now if I differ I risk becoming the laughing stock. In fact, had I been Galileo's contemporary, my thus theory of a limited horizon would probably have led to my incarceration. So many poets have showered praise on the ocean that my lack of reverence for it would not make any difference—at least to the ocean. The sea looks gorgeous when the waves swell up, but it is my misfortune that these very waves give me vertigo and a twisted outlook.

When I first ventured out of my cabin after those dreadful six days, my eyes fell on my co-passengers and theirs fell on me. It is in my nature that I feel more than a little intimidated by the class of humans known as *ladies*. Getting anywhere near them can lead to so many dangers that if the wise Chanakya were alive today he would advocate against venturing within ten thousand cubits of any of them. On the one hand, their proximity can cause many quite pitiable calamities in the kingdom of the heart. On the other hand, any misutterance in their presence can cause them to lose patience and be overcome with shame and revulsion at the breaking of the rules of etiquette. What if I develop mental confusion observing their elaborate gowns? What if I have to help them with carving meat during meals and what if I end up cutting my own finger in the attempt! Such were the concerns that kept me away from the ladies aboard that ship. Although there were plenty of ladies on the ship the gentlemen kept complaining that not one of them was suitably young or pretty.

I came to know many of the gentlemen on the ship. We came to know one Mr. B... particularly well. He is a prolific talker, a frequent laugher and has a great appetite. He seemed to know everyone and laughed in everyone's company. I consider it his virtue that he never measured his words and laughed hard at his own jokes be they meaningful or not. I grew to like him observing that he assigned no importance to his age or position, never measured his laughter or cared to tread the cautious middle path on controversial issues. This made him childlike and I am easily affected by the sagacity of a wise old man combined with childlike unworriedness. He referred to me as 'the angel' and called Mr. Gregory, 'Gorgori' (which sounds like the Bengali word for a hookah) and yet another passenger, 'the rohu fish', the only fault of the last among the list being that he had a very short neck. In fact it seemed he had no neck between his head and trunk—hence the unfortunate name-calling. Nevertheless, there obviously exists no simple explanation as to why I would be grouped with angels.

Mr. T... who was sailing with us is a novel kind of person. He is an intense philosopher. He never talked in colloquial language. In fact he never spoke; he lectured. One evening we were having a merry time on the deck when unluckily for us Mr. B... said to Mr. T..., "Look what a beautiful star". This elicited a serious philosophical discourse on the relationship between stellar bodies and human life reducing us to an ignorant audience.

There was a John Bull on board. His built was reminiscent of a palm tree, his mustache resembled a broom, his hair stood like quills on a porcupine, his face was a pot, his eyes were glassy like those of a fish. His presence filled me with awe and I always maintained a safe distance from him. Well, some people have a countenance suggestive of a guilty mind.

Every morning our John Bull would employ the services of all the languages known to him which included English, French and

Hindustani to swear at the subordinate members of the ship's crew, and create violent commotion. He never smiled and had no friends. He would sit by himself in his cabin and grimace. On some days he would stroll on the deck and whoever met his half-forgiving, half-devouring eyes was sure to be treated like a doormat.

Mr. B... always sat next to me at the table. He is a Eurasian who just like an Englishman has mastered the art of whistling and that of standing with his legs apart with his hands tucked into his pockets. He had a soft spot for me. One day he said to me somberly, "Young man, you're going to Oxford? Oxford is an excellent university". On another day, I was reading Trench's Proverbs and their Lessons when he came down whistling and took the book from me and after browsing a few pages very quickly, said to me, "Yes, a very good book!"

We sailed from Aden to Suez in five days' time. Those who take the route to England via Brindisi have to disembark at Suez and travel by train to Alexandria from where they sail to Italy. We being overland travelers disembarked at Suez likewise. Initially, four travelers including an Englishman, two other Bengalis and me co-hired an Arab vessel. If your eyes had happened to meet those of our bargeman you would have known how little divineness there is at times in the countenance of a man. His eyes were tigrine and his complexion was jet black, his forehead was low and lips thick. His expression was menacing. We bought his services because of a slight pricewise advantage. But Mr. B... was initially extremely reluctant to board this vessel. He said, "There is no trusting Arabs. They are quite prepared to stab you right in the neck!" He even cited one or two frightful examples of lawlessness in the Suez. Nonetheless we eventually boarded that boat. The bargemen speak precious little English. We sailed some distance without any hazard or trouble. The Englishman on board had some need of visiting the post office at Suez. The place being some distance from our route, our bargeman was not very eager to stop there. However, he agreed after some effort or so it seemed. Then a little while later he asked our co-passenger again, "Is it necessary to stop at the post office? It cannot be reached in a couple of hours!" At this the passenger got agitated and screamed at him, "Your grandmother!" And our bargeman matched his displeasure with a strong protest, "What? Mother? Mother? What mother? Don't say mother!" At this point some of us feared our co-passenger would presently be disposed of in the waters. The Arab asked him again, "What did say?" (sic). "Your grandmother!" returned the Englishman provoking the bargeman into almost attacking him. Realizing that he was in danger now the Englishman softened his stance and said, "You don't seem to understand what I say!" and went on to try and explain elaborately that the word 'grandmother' is not a swear-word. But then our bargeman roared something in his native tongue, something which seemed to say, "You're about to cross the limit. Shut up right now!" This dumbfounded the white man and he stopped talking for a length of time. Eventually, he asked again, "How far are we?" "Two shilling give, ask what distance!" (sic) thundered the bargeman. We realized that in the region of the Suez, if you pay no more than two shillings you might forfeit the right to make such inquiries. While our bargeman hollered at us thus, the oarsmen on the neighboring boats started exchanging glances and then grinning. Mr. Bargeman's crabbiness was evidently not something to savor with a straight face. On the one hand we were being hollered at and on the other the oarsmen had gradually begun guffawing. Finding no other means of avenging our dishonor the three of us took to venting our ire by laughing. There are times in life when we are forced to employ this kind of horse sense. Thus we barely made it to the city of Suez with our prestiges intact. I haven't earned the right to say anything about the city of Suez because I haven't ventured into more than half a mile of it. I had a desire to roam about there but those amongst us who had been to Suez before opined, "Such an enterprise would bring nothing but fatigue and disgust." While that didn't deter me I also learned that the only way to fulfill my desire would be to ride on a hired donkey. This served to weaken my wish, and I was further told that the donkeys of Suez do not always agree with those who try to ride them, they in fact have desires of their own; this produces conflict with the donkey's desire frequently triumphing in intensity over that of the one on top. In the city of Suez a deplorable affliction of the eyes is very much manifest. Hundreds of street-walkers go about with such diseased eyes, the fly being its vector. The flies collect the contagium from afflicted eyes and spread them when they sit on healthy ones.

In Suez, we boarded our train. The trains plying on this railroad have afflictions of their own. To begin with, there is nowhere you can lie down the seats being detached from one another and secondly the speed at which they locomote is seldom associated with trains. All night the train chugged on as we slept and we woke up next day to find ourselves all but buried in dust. When I attempted to feel my hair with my fingers I realized that my scalp had been blessed with a layer of topsoil suitable for cultivating rice. We arrived in Alexandria like hermits bathed in dry mud. The railroad was surrounded on either side by verdant crop fields. In these fields stood date palms bearing clusters of dates. In some places there were wells and here and there were scattered brick-houses. The brick-houses were square shaped sans pillars, sans porticoes, mostly walls with windows in between. This gave them a staid outlook. Nevertheless, this picture of Africa refused to tally with the Africa of my fantasies. My notion of Africa was uniform uncultivable desert-land. What I met instead, the date bowers amidst the green fields on that sparkling morning filled up my senses.

The steamer 'Mongolia' awaited us in the port of Alexandria. In boarding her we came to be borne on the Mediterranean Sea. It was a bit chilly. Right after boarding ship I bathed meticulously to rid my very bones of the dust I had collected. Following that I went on a tour of Alexandria. A small pinnace was hired to get us back on land.

The boatmen of Alexandria are so to speak each like a modern-day edition of Sir William Jones in that they speak several tongues including Greek, Italian, French and English even if only somewhat well. French is the native language of this port I was told. The names of streets and shop signs were mostly written in French. Alexandria presented itself as a city of affluence. There were people of so many ilks and shops of so many orders that they would be difficult to give an account of. The roads were paved in stone making them rather clean but at the same time noisy from the vehicles that plied on them. The houses and shops were all very spacious and the city looked gorgeous. The port of Alexandria is of a goodly size and provides shelter to the ships of several communities. Some of these ships belong to the European community, some to the Muslims, only none belonging to Hindus.

We reached Italy in four or five days time. It was one or two o'clock at night. We left our warm beds and packed up and arrived with our belongings on the roof of the ship. It was a full moon night and a very cold one at that. I was wearing insufficient warm clothing and felt very cold. Before us lay a very quiet city with all its doors and windows shut tightly—all fast asleep. Presently there was some confusion amongst us on board the Mongolia on the question of whether or not we would be able to avail a train. And what to do with our luggage? Would it be better to remain on board or should we proceed for the land? These were the questions whose answers we sought. An Italian officer appeared on board and started counting us although we hadn't the remotest idea why. Gradually there were rumors that this counting had to do with our prospects of boarding a train. As it turned out, we could not at all get on a train that night. Moreover, we came to hear that no train would be available till three o'clock in the afternoon creating considerable discontent amongst us. Finally we were put up for the night at a hotel in Brindisi.

That night I set foot on European ground for the first time in my life. Usually, when I arrive at a new destination I do so with such elaborate fantasies of newness that make the place look anything but novel to me. Everyone seemed surprised when they heard that I didn't think Europe was such a novel kind of place.

We arrived at our hotel in Brindisi at three o'clock at night and went straight to bed. In the morning we availed a decrepit carriage drawn by a half-dead horse to tour the city. The want of harmony between the coachman, his carriage and the horse that drew it was telling! Our coachman was about fourteen years old but his horse would be about fifty and the carriage was antediluvian. Brindisi is like any other smallish city. It has some brick-houses, some shops and streets. Beggars ask for alms, some people sit chatting in the pubs while others can be seen amusing themselves in the street-corners. No one is in a hurry for anything as if no one has anything to do nor has any concern. It would seem the whole city was holidaying. There was neither any significant traffic nor concourse of people. We had covered a little distance when a youth motioned our coachman to stop and climbed up with a watermelon in hand and sat next to him. "He has hopes for some easy money", said Mr. B... As our carriage rolled on, the stranger would point at "the church", "the garden", "the fields". This did not benefit us in terms of knowledge and its absence would have caused us no loss. No one had invited him to board our carriage, and none had asked him any questions, and yet we had to foot the bill for his unsolicited kindness. He and the coachman took us to an orchard with a huge variety of fruits. We found ourselves amidst clusters of grapes, some of them dark and the rest light colored. Of them I found the dark grapes to be sweeter. There were large trees bearing peaches and apples as well as other fruits. An old woman (probably the keeper of this orchard) appeared with some fruits and flowers. We did our best to ignore her, but she turned out to be a master fruit-seller and soon a bewitching lass approached us with a bouquet of fruits and flowers. This we failed to ignore. Italian women are very beautiful, somewhat like the women of my native land. They have beautiful complexion with black hair, black eyebrows, black eyes and very pretty faces.

We left Brindisi by the three o'clock train. On both sides of the railroad were beautiful grape plantations. We passed by all the riches of a poet's dream in the form of hills, rivers, lakes, cottages, crop fields and hamlets. How beautiful it is to watch a distant town emerge through the trees with its gradually nearing palace-tops, church towers and picturesque dwellings. At dusk I saw a resplendent lake at the base of a hillock. It was an unforgettable sight. The lake was surrounded by foliage and seemed to bear the shadow of the very evening—oh what beauty—I wouldn't succeed in describing it fully.

Our train passed through the famous tunnel within the Mont Cenis. When digging started, the French proceeded from one side of the mont and the Italians from the other and the diggers met about halfway through the tunnel a few years later. It took us just half an hour to cross this tunnel and the darkness made us a bit impatient. These trains have their lights turned on all the time because at places they pass through pitch dark caves every five minutes or so availing very little daylight for a stretch. We grew oblivious of the rigors of travel watching the cascades, rivers, hills, hamlets and lakes on our way from Italy to France.

Our train reached Paris in the morning. What a magnificent city! It is easy to lose oneself in its jungle of skyscrapers. Paris: where there are apparently no poor people. And the grandiose buildings—are they necessary for a human being of three and a half cubits? We went to our hotel which was palatial making me feel like I was wearing awkwardly loose-fitting clothes. Paris was astonishing with monuments, fountains, gardens, palaces, boulevards paved in stone, cars, horses and babel. We visited a Turkish bath. There we were first seated in a warm room where some of us started sweating, but not me. So I was given a warmer room. It was fiery and my eyes ached if I kept them open. I got out of that unbearable heat after just a few minutes and began sweating profusely. Then I was asked to lie down and a bare-bodied hulk started massaging me. I had never seen a man with such enormous muscles. The breadth of this man was reminiscent of a roscoe and he was no less a buffalo-shouldered, colossal Sal with goliath arms! Such a canon as this was not necessary for rubbing such an airy creature thought I. He said that I was quite tall and now if I grew sufficiently sideways I would be counted as a handsome man. After half an hour's non-stop massage it seemed to me that I had been cleaned of all the dust which my skin had gathered since I was born. Then I was taken to another room where I was thoroughly bathed and cleaned with warm water, soap and sponge. After this round I was taken to yet another room where they directed jets of hot water to my body. Then all of a sudden freezing cold water took the place of the hot jets. After bathing intermittently in hot and cold water for some time I entered a water machine where darts of ice-cold water fell on me from all six sides. After facing the ice-cold water-darts for some time, it seemed to me that the very blood inside my chest would freeze. I came out panting. Then they took me to the poolside and asked me if I would like to swim. I declined but my friend swam seeing which they started saying amongst themselves, "Look how strangely they swim, just like dogs." And now we were through with the whole affair of taking a bath. In conclusion, bathing in a Turkish bath is like sending your body to the washerman's. After our baths, we hired a car for the day for a pound sterling and we first headed for the Paris Exhibition. I see you have suddenly become quite eager to hear my discourse of it. But unfortunately, just like my studies at the university in Calcutta city, I have despite seeing the whole exhibition paid little attention to the details. We could not stay in Paris for more than a day and the Paris Exhibition is not something you can take in in a single day. We watched the exhibition all day long, but the exercise led to a thirst for seeing even more and one which remained unquenched. The exhibition is like a city by itself. Had I stayed in Paris for a month I might have ventured to pen a full description. The impression it left on my mind is in general chaotic and I lack an orderly memory of it. I do remember seeing many fantastic sketches and paintings. In the sculpture section I had seen numerous stone sculptures. There were exhibits from different parts of the world but I don't remember much of the complex details. Then we went to London from Paris. I have never seen a city so dark and dreary as this. London was smoky, cloudy, rainy, foggy and muddy and everybody seemed to be in a mad hurry. I was in London for only about a couple of hours—when I left it I heaved a sigh of relief. My friends said that London is not a place to fall in love with at first sight; one must stay in London for a few days to appreciate its true beauty.

My Second Letter

I came to England expecting rather foolishly to witness in every corner of this pint-sized island Gladstone's oratory, Max Müller's elucidation of the Vedas, Tyndall's scientific propositions, Carlyle's sublime thinking and Benn's philosophical treatises. Fortune favored me and I was disheartened to find that this was not the case. The womenfolk seemed largely occupied with their grooming; the menfolk were more involved in their work. For the English life flowed along its natural course, just that there was a lot of commotion about politics. I found that the women were more inclined to say things like did you go to the dance, how did you like the concert, there is a new actor at the theater, tomorrow a band will be performing and so on. And the men would say things like what do you make of the Afghan war, the Marquis of Lorne gained much popularity in London, today is an excellent day, yesterday was miserable. The women here play the piano, sing songs, enjoy a warm fireplace, read novels leaning on the sofa, make friends with visitors, and flirt with young men with or without believing it to be necessary. The spinsters are pretty active. They lend their voices to temperance meetings, working men's societies and all other functions and events.

They don't have to attend office like the men, nor do they have children to bring up. Besides they are frequently too old to spend all their time at the ball or flirting with young men. Consequently they have the time to do plenty of work which may be beneficial.

Here, almost every other door is a wine shop or a liquor shop. When I go out I see shoe stores, tailors, butchers and toy stores but precious few bookshops. We needed to purchase a poetry book but there being no bookshop in our neighborhood a toy-seller was sent to get it for us. In the past I held the notion that slaughterhouses and bookshops would receive equal importance in this nation.

In England, the first thing that catches your attention is the bustle. It is amusing to simply watch the worried countenances of the pedestrians swishing about umbrella under arm paying no attention to one another, perhaps afraid of losing out in the game of hide and seek versus time. There are railroads all over London and trains ply about once every five minutes. Other trains swooshed past above us, below us, beside us and on all sides of us during our train ride from London to Brighton. These trains have something in common with Londoners in that they too seem to be scurrying and panting. A visitor to this bantam nation is constantly afraid of taking one step too many and drowning in the sea! Heaven knows why they have so many trains. On one occasion we had perchance missed our train to London, but we did not go back to our rooms and boarded the next train which arrived half an hour later.

The people here are not nature's pampered babies and there is little scope for idling. Unlike our own country where you can till the land by scratching with an insignificant stick, here the farmers must battle winter to raise a crop. Firstly, they need lots of clothes to keep themselves warm and secondly, they must eat large quantities of food to enable their body to generate heat. They need an endless supply of clothes, coal, edibles and moreover alcohol. The food that we eat in Bengal is nominal and the layers of clothes that we wear are very few. Here, only the strongest can raise his head and those who are weak are also defenseless. On the one hand they have a war to wage against the elements and on the other they come across a thousand adversaries while making a living.

I gradually came to know a few locals. I noticed a funny thing that the locals invariably thought that I was very naive. One day I went out with Dr...'s brother. On our way there were a number of photographs in a shop window. He stopped me there and started explaining to me that those pictures were created with a kind of machine and were not hand-drawn. And we soon found ourselves at the center of a group of onlookers. Then there was a watch shop and he tried really hard to impress upon me that the clock is a marvelous machine. Miss... asked me at an evening party whether I had ever before heard the sound of a piano being played. Some people here may be able to map the celest but their knowledge of India is extremely limited. They also find it hard to imagine that other countries may be different from England. Even if you leave out Indology, the common people here are ignorant of many common things.

My Third Letter

The other day we went to a fancy ball attended by men and women in masks and costumes. The ballrooms were very big and lit with gas lights and there were bands playing music to six to seven hundred people. The place was chock-full of pretty faces. Men and women danced around hand in hand like pairs of lunatics. Each room was occupied by about seventy to eighty couples, with little space left. In one of the jam-packed rooms a champagne war was under way and there was plenty of meat on the tables. Some of the lasses would prance non-stop for two to three hours, tapping their feet without rest. One of the girls was dressed as an ice-maiden. She wore glittering white beads. Another went as a Muslim woman and her attire included a pair of flowery red long pants and baggy silken breeches. She was also wearing some sort of headgear and looked nice. Another was dressed as an Indian with a sari over her bodice and a wrapper over that and I think wearing that dress she looked better than how she might have looked in English clothes. Another went as an English maid. I dressed up as a Bengali feudal lord wearing clothes and a turban made of velvet and brocaded with glittering metallic threads. A certain person amongst us went as a

Talukdar—a kind of landholder with administrative powers—of Ayodhya. He wore white long pants made of silk and brocaded with metallic threads and a long robe and a long loose fitting outer garment made of white silk, and a turban and a cummerbund with metallic threads. The real Talukdars of Ayodhya may or may not dress this exact way but if they didn't, there was no one to point it out. One of us went as an Afghan chieftain.

Last Tuesday we were invited to a dance at the house of a gentleman. It is necessary to wear warm clothes for going out after dark but evening parties are an exception and clothes made of fine broad-cloth are the rule. The shirt must be spotless white. Over it is worn a black waistcoat made of broad-cloth and almost entirely open on the front side through which opening the white shirt shows. A white necktie embellishes the neck and over all this is worn a tail coat. The front side of the tail coat is absent from the bottom up to the waist. Unlike our loose fitting robes, the tail coat does not extend up to the knees. Since the front side is limited to the waist and above and the reverse side is not, the tail coat does remind one of a hanging tail of sorts. I thus wore this tail of a coat in imitation of the English. To go to a dance party a gentleman must also wear a pair of white gloves because if you don't then you may spoil the hands or gloves of the ladies while dancing. Everywhere else you must take off your gloves before shaking hands with a lady but in the dance hall the exact opposite is expected.

We arrived at their house at half past nine. The dance hadn't yet started. The hostess stood near the entrance shaking hands with well acquainted guests, nodding to others and welcoming everyone. In this white-dominated land, the host does not have an important role in entertaining guests invited to a banquet and may well be sleeping during the entire affair. We entered the house which was illuminated by gas lights but the lights looked moribund in contrast to the hundreds of sprightly beauties present there. What a pageant; it bedazzled my eyes! On one side of the room pianos, violins and flutes were playing. Couches and stools were placed close to the walls on all sides. The mirrors hesitated with the gas lights and the charming faces reflected on them. The floor of the dance hall was wooden and without a carpet. Its surface was polished to the point of being slippery to ease the gliding of feet while dancing. The balconies outside the dance hall were covered with foliage and provided with couches and stools. These were referred to as bowers and there the young men and women could engage in a bit of amorous communion when they were tired dancing or vexed by the din. Upon entry each guest was given a piece of paper listing the dances to be performed in gilded letters. There are two types of English dances, one in which a duet gyrate together, and another in which four or eight couples stand facing each other in a square formation and perform various maneuvers holding each others' hands. The former is called round dance and the latter is known as square dance. The hostess introduces the men to the women before the dance starts, that is, she approaches a lady accompanied with one of the gentlemen and says, "Miss..., this is Mr..." at which both nod politely. If the gentleman wishes to dance with a lady to whom he has been introduced, he takes out the program sheet and asks the lady, "So who are you going to dance this one with?" If she says, "No one" then the question follows, "May I have the pleasure of this dance?" If she thanks him that means she is willing and her name is written on the proposer's program sheet and his name is written on the lady's program sheet beside the gilded letters.

The dancing commenced. Round and round and round, about forty to fifty duets dancing in a single room; sometimes rubbing against each other, sometimes pushing, even colliding. But, round and round and round they go. The music playing in rhythm, feet tapping to the music, and the room warming up. A dance ends and the music stops. The dancer takes his tired companion to the banquet hall full of fruits, desserts and wines perhaps for a drink or a bite or perhaps to one of the bowers for some secretive romancing. When it comes to meeting new people I tend to be shy. I cannot even dance a dance at which I am a thorough expert if I am asked to do so with a lady I have just met. To tell you the truth I don't like these dance parties a lot. I do enjoy dancing with those whom I know very well. Just as in a card game people get very mad at inept partners, in a dance the women get very mad at bad dancers. I suppose my partner at the dance was secretly praying for my demise and when the dance ended both of us were greatly relieved.

When I had first entered the dance hall I was happily surprised to see a dusky Indian lady among those hundreds of whites. There was a flutter in my heart and I became eager to get acquainted with her. I hadn't seen a woman of her complexion in a considerable length of time! And her face exuded the soft and innocent nature of our Bengali girls. I had come across softness and innocence in the countenance of many an English girl but that is quite a different thing and the difference is not one which I can explain. Her hair was done in our native style. I now realized that I had grown a bit fed-up meeting white faces and immodest beauty. English women are completely different and I haven't become English enough to converse with them sans hesitation. Besides it takes courage to adventure beyond one's known frontiers.

Today, Brighton's prayers have been answered and the sun has shown his face. Here, no one stays indoors on a sunny day and the roads and the sea beaches are full of people. Although English houses do not have inner chambers, yet English women see the sun much less than Indian women do.

We don't rise before half past eight in the morning. If ever we decide to rise at six, the people here are surprised. Soon after rising I bathe in plain water, rather than making a mockery of taking a bath as people here do. I pour water directly on my head—not warm water but ordinary ice-cold water. Our breakfasts arrive at nine. Nine o'clock here is like six o'clock there. We eat our most important meal, the lunch at half past one. Between lunch and supper, we have tea with bread and then an elaborate supper at eight o'clock. These meals divide our day into major parts.

It's getting dark and it's almost four; after four it is impossible to read without lighting the lamps. Since we generally don't rise before eight o'clock the day really starts at nine. Add to that the darkness after four. The days seem to come and go like ten-to-four office workers. Daylight disappears before you can open the cover of your pocket watch. Contrariwise, the nights come on horseback but leave on foot.

There is no respite from clouds, rain, the wind and the cold. In our country rains tend to be heavy and noisy and accompanied by dense clouds, lightning and thunder and create quite a rush. Here, it's a different kind of rain—it's light and boring and it goes on and on in silent footsteps. The roads get muddy and the leafless trees get sodden in silence even if slowly. You can hear the slow pitter-patter of raindrops falling on window panes. In our country, layers of clouds are clearly visible. Here, it seems as if there are no clouds and it is just that the color of the firmament has somehow turned murky and all things mobile and immobile have together formed a gloomy outlook. Sometimes I hear reports like, "Yesterday we heard the sound of thunder". But apparently, the voice of the thunder itself is too meek to report firsthand. Here, sunshine is a thing heard of in rumors. If owing to tons of luck I happen to see the face of the sun on a morning, I remind myself –

This day will pass, know you not?

Day by day the temperature has been falling. Folks are saying that it may snow in a day or two. The thermometer has given a reading as low as 30 degrees—and that is about the freezing point of water. A little frost has also appeared. Dew drops have frozen to form very hard glass-like pieces on the streets. Somebody seems to have splattered small amounts of lime amongst the grass, the first signs of snow! It's very cold now and at times I have a chafing sensation in my hands and feet. Sometimes the thought of getting out of my quilt in the morning worries me. When we go out in the streets, some people laugh at our indigenous clothes while others are so stupefied that they temporarily lose their power to laugh. Many a pedestrian got nearly run-over because of our clothes. When we were in Paris, a bunch of school kids had run after us shouting. We saluted them. One of them started laughing out loudly while another shouted—"Jack, look at the blackies!"

My Fourth Letter

The other day we had been to the House of Commons. The Parliament's lofty tower, mammoth buildings and wide open rooms reminiscent of wide open mouths startled me. The House sits in a big hall with a gallery along its periphery on one side of which sit the audience and on the other newspaper reporters. This gallery is to an extent like the dress circle of a theater. The members sit in the stalls below the gallery. They are allotted a total of ten benches on two sides. Five benches on one side are occupied by members of the government and the five on the other side are occupied by members of the opposition. There's a chair on the platform in front, where the Speaker (resembling a president) sits wearing a wig and with it a very grave countenance. If anyone departs from decorum or law, the Speaker gets up and stops them. Women sit in a gallery behind Venetian blinds and cannot be seen from outside. When we entered the house, an Irish member called O'Donnell was delivering a speech on India. He was protesting The Press Act and some other things. His contention was not admitted. The culture of the House surprised me. While one member was delivering a speech many others were shouting, "Yeah, yeah,

yeah, yeah ..." and giggling. In our country, even school kids behave better than this at assemblages. Some members were sleeping with their hats extended to cover their foreheads. At one time when a speech concerning India was being delivered there were hardly nine or ten people inside the House and the rest had left to take a walk or eat. But when the time to vote came, everyone rushed in. It didn't seem that the voters' decision had anything to do with the speech on the subject or on any reasoning at all.

Last Thursday, there was a lot of sparring in the House of Commons over India. Mr. Bright submitted the petition of the Indians regarding Civil Service, taxes on the Gladstone variety of cotton and the Afghan war. The Parliament opens at four o'clock in the evening. A small group of Bengalis including me entered the House a little before that. Since the House hadn't yet opened the visitors were waiting in a large hall outside the house. Busts of great political exponents like Bark, Fox, Chatham and Walpole stood in that hall. The sentries guarding the doors wore hoary wigs. Some employees of the Parliament donned gowns and were going about with notebooks in their hands. The House opened at four. We had tickets to the Speaker's Gallery. The

House of Commons has five galleries, namely, Strangers' Gallery, Speaker's Gallery, Diplomatic Gallery, Reporters' Gallery and Ladies' Gallery. A ticket to the Stranger's Gallery can be obtained from any Member of the House, while the Speaker can give out tickets to the Speaker's Gallery. I'm not sure what the Diplomatic Gallery is because of the few times that I have been to the House I haven't seen more than one or two people in it. It is difficult to follow the proceedings from the Strangers' Gallery. In front of it is the Speaker's Gallery and in front of that the Diplomatic Gallery. We took our seats and the Speaker took his wearing his wig and consequently looking like the avian Garuda of mythology. The members took their seats and the proceedings commenced with the question-answer session. Members who have declared at the previous meeting of the House that they will ask questions on a specific topic at the next meeting can do so now. An Irish member named O'Donnell asked, "Is the government aware of the news published in The Echo and a few other newspapers about the atrocities of English soldiers against Zulus? And aren't such atrocities unbecoming of Christians?" Sir Michael Hicks Beach representing the government stood up at once and used some harsh words against

O'Donnell. At that all the Irish members stood up to answer Beach with equally harsh words. After quarreling over the issue for some time both sides finally sat down quietly. When the question-answer session ended and the speeches were to be delivered most of the members left the House. After about a couple of speeches, Bright stood up and submitted numerous petitions relating to the Civil Service. The elderly Mr. Bright attracts respect and his face seems to be the personification of generosity and kindness. Unfortunately for us, Mr. Bright did not deliver a speech on that day. Of the few members present in the house many had prepared to sleep, when Gladstone stood up. And as he stood up the whole House became silent and then hearing Gladstone's voice the members who had gone outside started returning and the benches were soon full. Gladstone's words emerged from the depth of fullness. He neither screamed, nor thundered, yet everyone present in the House could hear every word he uttered. Gladstone has a firm way of speaking so that his every word enters the depths of the hearer's mind and instils conviction. He would form a fist with his hand and lean towards a side while emphasizing a word as if he were wringing it out. And each such emphasized word seemed to enter the mind smashing its doors and windows. Although Gladstone spoke without stopping, all his words were measured and none of it was incomplete; he did not speak with uniform emphasis because if he did he would have antagonized his audience. He emphasized only the words which he thought needed emphasis. It is true that he speaks with verve but he doesn't shout and it seems whatever he is saying is his own firm belief.

When Gladstone ended his speech, the house became nearly empty with only six or seven people in the benches. By the time Smalet began his speech the benches were all but empty. But Smalet is not easily discouraged and he delivered an elaborate speech to the empty House during which I took a deep sleep. The one or two members who were still present were either gossiping or dreaming of becoming the Prime Minister after Disraeli's fall, their eyes covered with their hats. The Irish members of the House are a hapless lot. Whenever they stand up to make a speech the non-Irish members start quacking "Yeah, yeah ..." like ducks and the speaker's voice becomes inaudible in the banter. Being obstructed thus, the person delivering the speech loses self-control and gets very angry, and the angrier they get is the more they are laughed at.

However, these days Irish members have become vengeful. Whenever there is a discussion in the house, they do their best to obstruct it and whenever something is proposed they stand up one by one to disrupt the proceedings by making wanton rambling speeches.

My Fifth Letter

At this point I do not wish to dwell on what things capture the Bengali's attention upon arrival in England or their first impressions of the English society on the basis of my own experiences. This is because I feel I don't have the right to opine on these matters as the people who accompanied me to England and put me up here have been in England for a long time and are very well acquainted with the place. I have heard so much about England before setting foot on it that I found very little novelty on arrival. I did not face too many obstacles mingling in English society. So I think its not worth bothering you with my own experience. Let me instead tell you of the experiences of some other Bengalis staying in England.

A group of Bengalis boarded their ship from India. The first difficulty they faced was with the English attendants. Some of them would address the attendants with the word 'Sir' besides hesitating to give them orders to perform chores. During the entire voyage, they were very self-restrained about everything and this restraint was not just due to fear but also due to shyness. In whatever they did they were wary of breaking conventions. They kept away from the English on board being fresh from India where the Lords and Highnesses scorn natives and look away from them. Sometimes you may come across a very polite person from England who will try to make friends with you noticing your loneliness in the absence of your own folks. Such people tend to come from cultured and noble backgrounds. When the John, Jones or Harry wriggling about the bylanes of England like vermin alights on Indian soil, he becomes locally famous and when he rides a horse whip-in-hand (and that whip may not be solely for the horse) people scurry to make way; a signal from him is sufficient to shake up the throne of an Indian king; given all this I am not surprised that they develop bloated egos. If you give a horse and a whip to one who has never ridden, he may rain lashes on the horse trying to make it budge without knowing that a slight tug of the rein can achieve much more. But once in a while one comes across a good-natured white man who retains his humaneness amidst the highly infectious disease of Anglo-Indianism; who despite having been vested with draconian powers does not let pride get the better of him. Away from his native society and served by thousands, it is a trial by fire for the conscience of the humane Englishman.

Getting back to our group of voyagers, by now their ship has reached Southampton.

Thus they have reached Britain. They board a train for London and come across an English guard at the time of leaving train. The guard politely asks them what they need and soon arranges for porters and a car. The travelers think, "This is superb! We never knew that the English can be so polite." They do tip the guard with a shilling but a Bengali youth who has just arrived from India is more than willing to spend that money to be saluted even once by a white person. Those from whom I heard these stories have been living in England for many years and they do not well remember all their first reactions to England. They can recall only those things that left profound impressions on their minds.

Their friends living in England had arranged for their rooms prior to their arrival in England and upon entering these rooms they find to their horror a carpeted floor, paintings hanging from walls, a large mirror hanging at one place, a couch, beds, one or two flower vases, even a small piano. And their first reaction is something like, "Do you think we have come here to lead a life of luxury? We don't have much money and we cannot live in such an expensive place!!" The ones who had arranged for these rooms are quite amused at this protest for they had been so far oblivious of the fact that years back they themselves had reacted this exact way upon arriving in England. Regarding the new arrivals as rice-eating simpletons from Bengal they declare with a brushed-up air, "All the rooms in this place are like this". The new arrival mentally compares this to his native home—the humid room with a hard cot and over it a cheap mattress, smoking hookahs in groups here and there, two to four men playing chess after removing their shoes, each one wearing a loincloth, a cow leashed in the courtyard, cowpats drying on the brick wall with the washing hanging in the portico. The first few days they would hesitate to use the beds, couches and tables or to walk on the carpets. They would sit on the sofa leaning on one side lest it become soiled or get damaged in some way. It would seem to them that the sofas are kept for show and the landlord would not like them to be worn out with use. This was their first reaction upon entering an English dwelling; but I am yet to say something about another major subject.

Although it is a fact that English houses have landlords, it is the landlady that the tenant gets to see the most. Paying the rent, negotiating, arranging for meals are all transacted with the landlady. When my friends first arrived, an English lady came before them to wish them "Good morning" in a very unassuming tone. They got all worked up wondering how to return the politeness and after wishing her stood there stiffly. But when their other Anglo-Bengali friends started talking to her naturally, their wonder knew no bounds. Just imagine, a white lady with a pair of shoes, a hat, a gown! From that moment the new arrivals started regarding their friends very highly without thinking once that some day they too will develop the enormous courage to accomplish such a *feat*. After taking the new arrivals to their rooms the more experienced Anglo-Bengalis return to their apartments and joke about the ignorance of the inexperienced youths for a week or so. Every day the unassuming landlady would ask her tenants what they needed and they have told me that this gave them pleasure. One of them said he felt very happy all day long the first time he got an opportunity to upbraid the landlady a little bit. However, on that particular day, the sun did not rise in the west, nor did mountains walk or burning fires turn frigid without cause.

They have been living in luxury in carpeted rooms. They say, "In our native land, the concept of one's own room did not exist. While we sat in a room doing something, other members of the family would enter and leave the room in course of their everyday lives. I might be writing something while my older brother is snoozing close by with a textbook in hand and the tutor is teaching Bhulu multiplication tables loudly on a mattress laid on another part of the room. Here, I have my own room where I can arrange my books according to my convenience. I don't have to fear that some day a bunch of kids will run into them and demolish their order. Or that one day when I return from college at two o'clock three of my books will go missing and after a thorough search they will be found in the possession of my little niece who is busy showing her little friends pictures. Here you can stay in your room by yourself. Keep the door ajar. No one will enter your room without warning; they knock. The boys are not shouting or crying. Its perfectly quiet and trouble-free." And they begin to regard their native land with contempt.

It is frequently seen that our men do not mingle freely with Englishmen. It is so because here, in order to bond with male friends you need a kind of exuberance rather than occasionally answering "Yes" or "No" in a diffident contralto. But the Bengali expatriate can indeed mingle with women at the dining table uttering a few soft and sweet words to her ears and his joy in sitting beside her and talking to her is evident from his hair ends down to the tips of his boots. Having left our native land where beauty is veiled and confined to the house's inner chambers and having arrived in this land of candid beauty our hearts sing out like the moonbeam-drinking curlew.

One day one of our Bengali friends had gone to his first English dinner invitation. Foreigners customarily receive plenty of hospitality at such gatherings. The host's daughter took his arm and they sat at the dinner table. We don't get to mingle with our native women freely, moreover having come here recently it is difficult to be sure of the intentions of the local women. When they talk to us and laugh with us as part of socializing we assume that they have taken to liking us particularly. Our Bengali youth told the young Miss... many things about India. He said he liked England very much and does not wish to go back to India where the people are very superstitious. Finally he even told her a few lies like he almost got killed during a tiger hunting expedition in the Sunderbans. The young Miss easily understood that the youth had fallen in love with her. Pleased with her conquest she began shooting her sweetest words to his breast. What sweet conversation! In comparison to a hard-earned simple "Yes" or

"No" from one of our native women which is so soft that it disappears even before coming out of the veil; what flow of nectar from what red lips which enters the veins unasked like wine.

I suppose you can by now understand under the influence of what spices a substance known as 'The Bengali' is gradually transformed into a khichri which may be called 'The Anglo-Bengali'. I haven't been able to the give you all the details. The human mind is subject to so many minor influences that delving into every aspect would lengthen my writing enormously.

To understand Anglo-Bengalis fully, one must see them in three states—in the presence of the English, in the presence of Bengalis and in the presence of other Anglo-Bengalis. In the presence of the English they are pictures of demureness. Their politeness prevents them from straightening their necks, when they debate they do so as meekly as possible and regret that they had to debate at all and ask for forgiveness a thousand times. Even when they don't speak a word their body language speaks for them and their postures and countenances express their deep regard and modesty. But observe the same individual in the presence of other Anglo-Bengalis. The first thing you will notice is their rudeness. If that individual has been in England for three years he considers himself far superior to one who has been here for just one year. And if the two happen to quarrel, you will see the contempt with which the former treats the latter. He utters each word with such force and tone as if the rightfulness of his contention has been decided for good at an audience between him and the goddess of learning, Saraswati. The protester is squarely told that he is "just wrong" or even "uneducated".

The other day I heard one of them say that another Bengali had asked him, "What is your occupation?". On hearing this one of our Anglo-Bengali friends commented with evident repugnance, "How barbarous!" His implication seemed to be that just as stealing and lying are fundamentally unethical, so is asking a person about their occupation.

Once we were discussing our rituals of mourning, how we eat the self-prepared simple rice for a period following the death of a parent, and how we avoid dressing luxuriously for that same period. An Anglo-Bengali youth said to me impatiently, "You, of course do not like these rituals." I replied, "Why not? I see if the English would eat the mourning rice upon the death of a kin and we would not, then you would hate our native country twice as much and blame all our misfortunes on not partaking of the mourning rice." You may have heard that the English believe that if thirteen people eat at a table then one of them will surely die within a year. When an Anglo-Bengali invites guests he makes sure not to seat thirteen people together saying, "I don't believe it myself but have to follow this tradition lest my guests are overcome with fear." One day I saw an Anglo-Bengali prevent a young boy belonging to his family from playing in the streets on a Sunday. When I asked him why he did that, he answered, "What will the people outside think?"

Some Bengalis want to start the practice of renting apartments in India in the same way as is done here. That's all they want. Another Bengali wishes to reform Indian society having been greatly impressed by how men and women dance together in England. He has been fussing childishly about certain things noticing the dissimilarities between English and Indian women regarding some frivolous matters. One Anglo-Bengali complained that Indian women can't play the piano and they don't receive visitors or return visits. In this way their habitually ill-tempered apparatuses get red hot and their blood boils at all the slight differences between the two countries. An Anglo-Bengali was recently heard saying before his sympathizing friends that when he thinks of returning to India and of all the lachrymose women who will be surrounding him there, he no longer wishes to go back. In other words he wants his wife to come running to him at his very sight crying "Dear Darling" and to hug and kiss him and stand resting her head on his shoulder. It inspires reverence to watch these youth research over the correct fashion of holding forks and knives at the table. They seem to be dead right about what's fashionable and what's out of fashion when it comes to the design of coats, the tightness of pants as worn by the nobles, waltz versus polka-mazurka and meat after fish or fish after meat. The Bengali living in England fusses much more than the English about such petty conventions. If you use a knife to eat fish an Englishman will not be very surprised because he knows that you are a foreigner but an Anglo-Bengali will promptly ask for smelling salt. If you drink Champagne in a glass used to drink Sherry an Anglo-Bengali will stare at you as if your ignorance is about to destroy all the peace and happiness of the world. If he were a magistrate and you happened to be wearing your morning coat in the evening you would surely be jailed. On seeing a compatriot eating mutton with mustard seeds a certain person who had lived in England for some time and then returned to India had asked, "Then why don't you walk on your head?"

I've noticed another strange thing that the extent to which Bengalis criticize their motherland in the presence of the English far surpasses any criticism from any Indophobic Anglo-Indian. He brings up the topic himself and has a hearty laugh at the superstitions prevalent in India. He proclaims that among the Vaishnavites in India there is a sect named after Ballavacharya and describes all their ceremonies. He also caricatures Indian nautch girls and is pleased if he can get a few laughs. It is his intense desire not to be counted as an Indian and he is constantly afraid of being identified as a Bengali. Once a Bengali was going somewhere when another pedestrian approached him and asked him something in Hindustani. This angered him and he went away without replying. He doesn't like it when people can tell from his appearance that he speaks Hindustani. An Anglo-Bengali has written an 'anthem' to be sung in Ramprasad's style. I have previously quoted a few lines from this song but now that I remember the remaining lines let me write them down here for you. However, the writer unlike Ramprasad is not a worshiper of the dusky Shyama but a devotee of the fair Gauri whom he had addressed in his song –

"Mother, when I depart this life
I wish to be reborn a white man;
And place a hat on my red hair,
get rid of the libelous 'native' tan.
I'll hold white hands and
I'll go for walks on the lawn
(And) When I see a black face I'll scream
'Darkie' with scorn."

I have already mentioned English landladies and how they take care of their tenants. If they happen to have many tenants they employ a caretaker or engage their relatives in the work. Some tenants rent an apartment after making sure they find their landlady attractive. On entering their apartment they make friends with the youthful daughter of their landlady. In a day or two she gets a pet name and perhaps a poem in about a week's time. Once a landlady's daughter brought her tenant a cup of tea and asked him if he needed sugar to which he replied with a smile, "No Nellie, since you have touched the cup I don't see any need for sugar". I know an Anglo-Bengali who used to call his domestic helps older sisters. And I know one who was so devoted to them that if one of them was present in his room or the next one and one of his Anglo-Bengali friends broke into a song or laughter, he would chastise them saying, "Stop, stop! What will Miss Emily think?" I remember we once treated a person who had returned from England. During the meal he said with a sigh, "This is the first time that I'm partaking a meal without a lady at my table." An Anglo-Bengali had once invited his friends. At the table were seated the landlady and a few maids. Noticing that one of them was wearing dirty clothes the host requested her to change to which she replied, "If you love someone you can love them in dirty clothes just as well."

Now let me tell you about a virtue of the Anglo-Bengalis. Many of those who come here do not admit being married because married men are of lesser value amongst the maidens. One can have a nice time with the English maidens by pretending to be unmarried, but if you are known to be married your unmarried friends won't let you beat them; hence the advantage of pretending to be a bachelor.

You will of course meet many Anglo-Bengalis who do not fit the description I have supplied. But I have given you the general symptoms observed in the case of Anglo-Bengalis.

I have no significant knowledge about what happens to Anglo-Bengalis when they go to India. But I have seen plenty of what happens when they return to England after a stay in India. They tend to develop a dislike for England and are at a loss as to what or who has changed, they themselves or England. In the past they would be mesmerized with everything English; now they don't like the English summer or rains, and they are not sorry if they have to return to India. They say they used to like English strawberries very much and used to think that the strawberry is the tastiest fruit they have eaten. But now strawberries don't taste the same any more. Now it seems to them that many Indian fruits taste way better than strawberries. In the past they were very much fond of the creams made in Devonshire but now they are more fond of Indian thickened cow-milk. They tend to settle down in India with wife and children and start earning. They become more easygoing and are happy to spend the day fanning themselves. In contrast, in England you need a lot of enthusiasm to have fun or lead a life of luxury. Here there are no cars to ferry you from one room to the next, so to say, and it is not practicable to depend on ten servants to mobilize you. Fares are quite high and servants cannot be kept by dispensing three and a half rupees a month. If you want to watch a theater, and its raining in the evening then you must walk a mile through the mud, umbrella over shoulder to reach there on time. These things can be accomplished only as long as one is sufficiently youthful and vigorous.

My Sixth Letter

Our house in Brighton is in a secluded area by the sea. It's part of a row of twenty to twenty-five houses collectively referred to as the Medina Villas. I had expected to find a real villa with a big garden. When I arrived I found that all that the property had to show to be called a villa were a few trees growing in a few yards of land in front of the building. An iron knocker hung at the door of entrance. I rattled it a couple of times and the landlady opened the door. The rooms here are a lot smaller than those of my native land in terms of length, breadth as well as height. All the windows are shut tightly preventing the entrance of air through them but being made of glass they at least permit light. Small rooms of this kind are suitable for living in the winter season, you only have to light a small fire to warm it up. But on a cloudy day, when there isn't much light, and the rain slowly plip-plops all day long and when this happens for three or four days at a stretch without respite, I get very listless and it seems to me that time has come to a standstill. And not just me, for my English acquaintances say that on such days they feel like swearing (a purely European disease with no Bengali name) and their state of mind becomes irreligious. Anyway, the houses here are very clean, once you enter a house you won't see any dust, the floors are fully carpeted and the stairs are spic-and-span. The people here cannot stand any outward ugliness. Every small thing must look capital. Even mourning dresses have to look good. But cleanliness as we know it is an altogether different thing. The locals don't rinse after taking food because if you do, rinsed water dripping from your mouth looks very ugly. Ablution being ugly is avoided. Given the number of people who suffer from cough and cold a spittoon would do a room a lot of good but since spittoons are ugly the handkerchief takes over its job. Cleanliness as it is known in our country permits us to keep a spittoon in the room but bearing such a terribly dirty thing in our shirt-pocket is unthinkable. But here appearances rule. That no one gets to see the dirty handkerchief is considered good enough. The hair must be done neatly. The face and the hands have to be clean and that is enough, there is no need to bathe. Since people don't go out in shirtsleeves the only parts of the shirt visible are the chest and the cuffs. There's a kind of shirt from which the visible parts can be separated and reattached so that when the shirt gets dirty, instead of sending all of it to the laundry you can just remove the detachable parts and replace them with clean ones. The maids here have a piece of cleaning cloth tied to their waist with which they clean anything that needs cleaning. The shining plate on which you are served food is cleaned with the same piece of cloth but there's no harm in that because it doesn't look bad. People here are not unclean, they are what we term 'dirty'. And part of the reason behind it is the chilling cold. We don't consider anything to be clean unless they are washed with water. Here it isn't practicable to wet your hands so often. Besides because of the cold, things remain usable for longer periods on their own. And because of the cold and the layers of clothes, most of the skin is not easily exposed to dirt. Things don't rot as quickly. This kind of cleanliness does have at least some advantages. On the other hand, while we have elaborate cleaning rituals we also have many lapses. In our country, there's not a thing that is not disposed of in ponds. We bathe but bathe in polluted water-bodies; a massage of oil and a couple of dips make us habitually feel clean. We maintain cleanliness of our bodies and foods, but we don't clean our homes. We even make them unhygienic.

We began forming acquaintances in England. Dr. M... is a semi-old man in the business of medicine. He is a true Englishman and dislikes anything and everything that is not English. For him this tiny island is the world and his imagination has never crossed The Strait of Dover. He has so little imagination that he cannot grasp how people who do not regard the Ten Commandments of the Bible may desist from lying. His main contention against non-Christians is that if one is neither English nor Christian, how can such a creature be humane. His motto is, "Gladly he would learn and gladly teach", but I found that he has a lot to learn and not much to teach. His knowledge of English literature is surprisingly limited; he acquires bits of knowledge by reading a few monthlies. He cannot imagine how an Indian may be educated. Women here use a kind of round hairy thing called muff to keep their hands warm in winter. When I first saw this wonderful thing I had asked Dr. M... what it is and he was thoroughly shocked at my ignorance. In fact this is a common malady here, that people expect us to know every minute detail of English society. Once I had gone to a dance where a girl asked me, "How do you like the bride?" "Who is the bride?" I inquired. A number of ladies were present there and I did not know who the bride was. She expressed great surprise and said, "Do you not identify her from the orange flower on her head?"

I met a couple of Miss. K...'s who are daughters of the local clergyman. They look after the families of the neighborhood day and night, organize Sunday school, hold temperance meetings for the laborers and sing to keep them in good spirits. We being foreigners, they took very good care of us. If there was a merry gathering within the town they would inform us, they would even take us there, when they had spare time they would come to converse with us, sometimes they would teach the boys to sing, sometimes we went with them for a walk. Thus we received their care and attention. The older Miss. K... is very kind and rather quiet. She is slow and hesitant in answering questions. Her answers tend to be like, "Yes —no—may be—don't know". Sometimes she is at a complete loss for words or stops in mid-sentence, not sure what to say next. She isn't prompt in expressing her opinion. If someone asked her, "Do you think it will rain today?" she would say, "How would I know." She doesn't understand that she is not being asked for the gospel truth. She is reluctant to guess or estimate. I have never seen anyone as merry and unperturbed as the younger Miss. K... It would seem that she has never been upset or affected by anything. She is very virtuous, always very happy and loves to talk. She wears inexpensive clothes, is unpretentious and very simple.

One evening we were invited to Dr. M...'s house. Here food is not the main objective of holding a gathering. People get together to know each other, to play music and to dance, and to have fun. We arrived there in the evening. Some men and women were gathered in a small room. Upon entering the room we paid our obeisances to the host and the hostess. Greetings were exchanged as we were introduced to the other guests. There were so many guests and so little space that there was a shortage of seats. Most of us men were standing. Whenever a lady entered the house the hostess or the host would introduce her to us and we would stand or sit by her side for a while and exchange a few words, most of it starting with the weather. For instance, the lady says, "Dreadful weather!" with which I am in complete agreement. Then she conjectures that this kind of weather must be particularly trying for Indians and hopes that it will clear up soon and so on. Then we discuss many more things. There were two particularly beautiful ladies among the guests. It goes without saying that they knew that they were beautiful. Here, beauty is worshiped and cannot remain self-ignorant; self-admiration cannot be concealed and is aroused by admiration pouring in from all corners. In the dance hall beauty is at a premium; everyone wishes to dance with the prettiest girl; many are ready to do her bidding at the drop of a hat. Handsome men also have many takers and they are the drawing room darlings. I see that you will be tempted to come here hearing this. If a handsome man like you comes to a place where beauty is so worshiped, then there will be echoes –

> ... *heaves, like gales,*
> *tears like the rain,*
> *thunder-like wail–*

The two aforementioned ladies were the most beautiful people at the invitation even if wallflowers. The younger of the two sat leaning on a couch while the other occupied a seat by the wall. A couple of us were delegated the task of keeping them amused. Unfortunately I'm not great with conversations, not what they term 'bright'. Until now the host was waiting to make a request of a rather vain musician lady to play music. She was the oldest of the women present there and she was wearing more makeup than anyone else. She wore as many rings as her ten fingers could hold.

If I were the host I would know from her rings that she wished to play the piano. When she finished playing the piano the hostess began pleading with me to sing something. I knew I was in a difficult situation because the people here are not very much in love with our music. And one of the disadvantages of being well-behaved is that you cannot save yourself from becoming the laughing stock. So Mr. T... cleared his throat a couple of times as a prologue to his performance and then everyone became silent. I somehow managed to finish the task I had been given. The ladies were so amused that it was difficult for them to be polite. Some of them coughed instead of laughing, some pretended to have dropped something so that they could lower their head and suppress their laughter, one hid her face behind her friend's back finding nowhere else to hide, and those who had managed to appear relatively sober were telegraphing each other with their eyes. The elderly musician lady who had played the piano wore a faint disdainful smile which made my blood lose all its vitality. When my song ended my face and ears had colored; the room was abuzz with praises but I ignored it after so much laughter. The younger Miss. H... requested me to translate the lyric and I obliged. The first line went like this "Tell me not of love". Hearing the translation she asked me, "In your country, are people free to love?" The hostess started showing some guests a collection of photographs they had of the ruins of Rome. Dr. M... had purchased a telephone and was satisfying the curiosity of some of his guests about the instrument. Supper had been laid out in the next room. From time to time the host would discreetly ask a gentleman to take Miss. or Mrs. so-and-so to supper. The gentleman would ask the lady's permission to take her to supper and take her to the table in the next room accepting her arm. In this kind of a gathering, everyone invited do not eat together, because if they did then all the merry-making would almost stop. In such manner we men and women together spent an evening with music, conversation, fun and food.

Here there are numerous occasions for meeting between men and women. Dinners, balls, conversazioni, tea-parties, lawn parties, excursions, picnics etc. Thackeray says, "English society has this eminent advantage over all others—that is if there be any society left in the wretched distracted old European continent—that it is above all others a dinner-giving society." Spending a spare evening now and then dining and amusing themselves in the company of friends is the duty of an English family. Giving a description of such a dining hall here would be overkill. The difference between a dinner party and the party at Dr. M...'s which I have described is in matters of the right hand (although in this land of barbarians food is taken with both hands). Once I went on a boat ride as part of a picnic party. The boat ride was an enterprise on the part of the members of a local Sunday club. The members of this club including both ladies and gentlemen are against observing Sundays. And so they get together every Sunday for some innocent fun. Mr. M... a Bengali member of this club and our friend kindly gave us tickets for the boat ride. We took a train from London to a village by the Thames. On reaching there I found a large boat, and about fifty to sixty men and women who were against observing Sundays. The daylight was weak, the sky was overcast and all the invitees hadn't turned up. I myself wasn't eager to join this party, but Mr. M... very much wanted me to join it. A number of Indians were present there, I suppose Mr. M... may have tempted them by saying that there were attractive ladies in the group because all of them were very well groomed. Many of them had tied red nooses to their necks. Mr.

M... himself stuck a sword-shaped pin to his necktie. One of us asked him jokingly, "Is this to signify that all the ties in the country have been attacked with swords?" Mr. M... replied with a smile, "Not really. It's a sign of the knife of insinuation which has bloodied my bosom." But he didn't explain if the knife had bloodied him in his own country or here. Mr. M... never tired of banter; he spent that entire day gamboling and frolicking with everyone on that steamer. Once he started 'reading' the palms of the ladies and they laughed so much that to tell you the truth I was feeling a little jealous of him. The boat journey started at the expected time. The river was almost as narrow as our canals. We came to know one another and conversed on the steamer. One of us Indians had a debate with a English national on religion. I met a person who is very devoted to Shelly's poetry and being a lover of Shelly's poetry myself I was invited to visit their home. This person had studied English literature and politics in depth but did not know much about India. Once when we mentioned India he asked, "Under which king?" I answered a little surprised, "The British government" the reply to which was, "Yes I know that but directly under which king?" That's the limit of their knowledge about Calcutta. Feeling a little embarrassed, the reveler said, "Please excuse my ignorance, we should have known a lot more about India but I am ashamed to say that I know very little." Thus our conversation progressed on the roof of the boat, a tent-like covering over our heads. The tent gave us partial protection from the occasional plip-plop rain. I opened my umbrella leaving the ladies on the part protected from the rain. In the meantime our compatriot Mr. K... had taken shelter with the ladies. Later, upon our teasing him he said his only goal was to stay dry. This we took with a pinch of salt. Anyway, that day we were drenched in rain three or four times and we reached our destination soaking in rain. When we got off, the rain had ceased but the sky was still overcast and the soil wet. We had a plan to lunch on the grass, but had to abandon it because of the weather. After eating on the boat some of us got out for a stroll. Some amorous couples took out small oar-boats and still others went for secluded walks on the grass holding hands and whispering to each other. There was a photographer with us who took a picture of the entire group standing in a field. Suddenly Mr. M... decided that a photograph should be taken of all the dark complexioned people in the group. Some of us hesitated as they were opposed to such an invidious distinction. But

Mr. M... was not one to let go easily. Finally, our steamer left for London. Then the Sun-god having contained his thousand rays laid out his tired head on the bed of multitudinous clouds leaning on sunset's shadowy peak and closed his sleepy crimson eyes; the birds returned to their respective nests. The lowing herd headed for the cow-house tracing the cowboy's steps. We began our journey for London.

My Seventh Letter

Let me tell you a bit about the rich and fashionable ladies here. A couple of days at the hands of our ancient mother-in-law or widowed sister-in-law can fix them. These ladies are the daughters and wives of the fat cats. They have servants, they don't have to work, they have a housekeeper to supervise all the housework, they have a nurse to look after the children and a governess for additional help with them like their education; so there's nothing really left to do in terms of work. One thing remains though, and that is their grooming but for that there's a lady's maid so they don't have to do all of it by themselves either. They have the whole day at their disposal. The first thing they do to shorten their day is to lie in bed all morning with all the doors and windows closed so as to prevent any interference from sunlight. They eat breakfast in bed and if they manage to leave bedroom before eleven they think they have risen sufficiently early. Then comes dressing up about which I am unable to give you any details. I've been told that bathing has recently become fashionable in England but the fashion is yet to become widespread. They wash only the visible parts of the arms, the face and the neck many times a day; they don't worry about cleaning the rest of the body since the face is the most attractive part of a woman and its care is considered sufficient. They deem taking sponge-baths twice a month to be good enough. For a while I went to live with an English family and they were alarmed to hear that I bathe. They had no arrangements for bathing and a shallow tub was borrowed for my use.

When they have guests, the hostess's job is to converse with them and if there are many guests she must be careful to distribute her oration and her ambrosial smile evenly without favoring anyone particularly. This is a very difficult thing to do and must be the result of plenty of practice. I've noticed that they maintain eye contact with a person while speaking to them and as soon as they finish they turn towards everyone to smile. Or sometimes they start talking making eye contact with the listener and as they talk they take a quick look at each one present. Sometimes they deal a quick word to each guest just like an expert dealer quickly deals a deck of cards. They do it with such panache that it becomes apparent that they carry a number of ready-to-use sentences like cards in their repertoire. For instance the hostess says to a guest, "Lovely morning, isn't it?" and then quickly turns to another to say, "Yesterday night, Madam

Nielson sang in the music hall; it was exquisite!" And the lady visitors present start contributing an adjective each; one says "charming", another says "superb", yet another says "something unearthly" and one remaining just says "isn't it?" In my view these are conversational acrobatics practiced in the morning. And so she frequently has visitors. She is subscribed to the Moody's Library and short-lived novels keep making trips between the library and her residence where she ingests them continually. Then there is flirting; exchanges of sweet smiles and sweet words, pretending to be hurt over pretend pretexts, perhaps a joke or two from the gentlemen, and from the other side a delicate fist raised over sweet disgrace with a "Oh, you naughty, wicked, provoking man!" bringing complete gratification to the naughty man. Thus they welcome guests, return visits, read new novels, create fashion and fall victim to it, and along with that they flirt sweetly and perhaps 'love' among their daily tasks. Just as girls in our country are prepared for marriage from childhood and are not educated sufficiently because they won't go to office to work, here too girls are polished from childhood for selling at exorbitant rates and whatever education is needed to get them married is considered sufficient. A girl can be prepared for display in a shop window of the wedding marketplace by teaching her a little singing, a little piano-playing, graceful dancing, some French even if with distorted pronunciations, a little knitting and a little sewing. The difference between the girls of our country and those of this country is no more than the difference between an indigenously manufactured doll and an English doll. The girls of our native land don't need to play the piano and sundry skills and even English girls have to have a little education, but both are prepared for selling. Here also the males dominate and the women follow them faithfully; ordering the wife around and taking decisions on her behalf are considered rights granted by the Almighty. England has many types of women other than fashionable women, or otherwise things wouldn't add up. Women from middle-class households have to work hard and cannot lead a life of luxury. Every morning they have to inspect the kitchen, check if it's clean, whether they have supplies, whether such supplies have been kept in their proper places etc. Then they give orders to buy edibles and cooking ingredients from the market, improvise ways of saving money as a middle-class wife should, cook a soup from yesterday's leftovers if there be any, or bring stale remnants of meat from the day before yesterday to today's table after adequate transformation, and perform myriad other wifely feats. Then she has to play the role of a tailor for her children making stockings and other clothes as well as making clothes for herself. Not all of them are destined to read novels, but may be the newspaper. Some don't read newspapers either, they just read and write letters and read shopping bills and calculate expenditures. They say, "Let the men deal with politics and other weighty stuff. We have our own duties." Since weakness is a matter of pride for women, many can be seen leaning long before they tire. The same applies when it comes to matters of learning and they brag, "We don't understand all these things." Lack of education or intellect are things to be openly boasted about. The middle-class women here are not keen about education, and their husbands are none the unhappier for it; their lives revolve around their duties. Every evening, when the husband returns from work he earns a 'sweet kiss' (it goes without saying that depending on the family there are exceptions to this rule). He comes home to a warm fireplace and a ready meal. Perhaps the wife resumes her sewing in the evening and the husband starts reading out a novel for her. They have a fire burning, the room is adequately warm, it's raining outside and the doors and windows are tightly shut. Perhaps the wife plays the piano for the husband. Here middle-class wives are quite simple. Although they are not highly educated, they have knowledge of many different things, and their intellect is amply clear. In this country, one can learn a lot from conversation and they are not confined to the inner chambers of the home. They meet friends. They listen and voice their opinions if there is a discussion among their relations on an elevated subject. They can grasp how intelligent people examine the many different aspects to a subject from many different angles. So if a topic comes up they don't ask childish questions, nor do they stare in bewilderment. They can hold relaxed conversation with their friends, they are not grim or engulfed in shame at gatherings, they don't get improperly close with their acquaintances, nor are they unsociably distant. They are cheerful and content in society. They may not have extraordinary wit but have a great sense of humor and can enjoy a joke well-told with unbridled laughter. When they like something they also appreciate it without reservation.

Tagore

I lived with my teacher's family for some days. Theirs is a very unusual family. Mr. B... is a middle-class man. He is thoroughly versed in Latin and Greek and he has no children. The four people who lived in that house were his wife, their maidservant, he himself and me. Mr. B... is middle-aged and a gloomy figure who fusses a lot. He spends his time in a ground-floor room next to the kitchen. That room has small windows and its door he keeps shut. On the one hand the room has the potential to receive precious little sunlight and on the other he hangs a curtain over the window. The room and its walls are covered by formidable-looking old dusty torn Greek and Latin books of various sizes. One feels a little breathless on entering the room. This room is his study where he reads and teaches. His countenance always expresses disgust. If it takes him too much time to put on his tight boots he gets mad at them. When his pocket get caught in a nail fixed to the wall he furrows his eyebrows and twists his lips in anger. And just as he is fussy, Murphy gives him numerous opportunities to fuss. He stumbles as he walks, his chests refuse to open, and when it opens he doesn't find what he has been looking for. On some mornings when I come to his study I find him moaning and grimacing without any

77

apparent reason and all by himself. But Mr. B... is in fact an innocent gentleman. He's fussy but not short-tempered. He complains but does not quarrel. He does not vent his anger on humans but on his dog named Tiny. He yells at Tiny for moving and kicks him day and night. I've never seen him smile. He wears dirty and tattered clothes. This is how he is. He used to be a clergyman and I am ready to vouch that every Sunday he demonstrated the horrors of hell to his congregation. He is always so buried in work and has so many students to teach that some days he misses dinner. On some days he is busy right from waking up to eleven o'clock at night. Under such conditions, it is not at all surprising that he fusses. His wife is very inculpable, not angry or bold. She may have been beautiful at one time and looks older than she is, wears spectacles and does not dress up richly. She cooks and does the household chores and being childless does not have a lot of things to do. She used to take very good care of me. It is easy to see that the couple are not in love, but nor do they fight and the years pass by in silence. Mrs. B... never enters her husband's study and the only time they meet in the whole day is at the table and they don't talk to each other when they eat although they talk to me. B... needs potatoes so he says to his Mrs. in a hushed tone, "Some potatoes" (leaving out the word please or saying it inaudibly). Mrs. B... says, "I wish you were a little more polite". B... says, "I did say please". Mrs. B... says, "I did not hear it" and B... says, "It was no fault of mine". At this point they both fall silent. I found these situations very embarrassing. One day I was a little late at dinner and when I arrived at the table I found Mrs. B... upbraiding B... for taking too many potatoes with his meat. Mrs. B... stopped on seeing me and Mr. B... taking this as an opportunity for revenge began taking even more potatoes with his wife just staring at him angrily. Neither of them addressed the other as "Dear Darling", not even by mistake. Nor did they use their Christian names, they addressed each other as Mr. B... and Mrs. B... At times Mrs. B... would be conversing with me when Mr. B... would arrive and the conversation would stop. Both of them were like this. One day Mrs. B... was playing the piano for me when Mr. B... entered and asked, "When are you going to stop?" Mrs. B... says, "I thought you had gone out" and the piano stops. When I wanted to listen to the piano she would say, "I'll play it when that horrid man won't be in the house" and I would feel embarrassed. Thus the two were not in agreement and yet life went on. Mrs.

B... cooks, does the household work, Mr. B... earns the money; they never exactly quarrel although they tend to differ in opinion and that too so softly that the man in the next room cannot hear it. However, I stayed there for some days and after being embarrassed on many occasions on account of their disagreements I was glad to leave the house.

My Eight Letter

We have moved out of London. Do you know that the sea of humanity that is London has its ebb and flow? London has its high tide from the beginning of the spring season up to mid-summer. In this period it is chock-a-block with theater, song and dance, open and family balls; packed with fun and entertainment. The pleasure-seeking rich maidens make night seem like day. Today they have an invitation to a dance, tomorrow a ball, the day after tomorrow a theater, the next day Madam Patti's singing and so they are busier at night than during the day. Pretty lasses whom hundreds of admirers are more than willing to serve—moving the seat, advancing the plate, opening the door, helping them with carving meat, picking up the hand-fan—they dance all through the night without rest from nine to four o'clock in halls warmed by gas-lights and people breathing. They are not like our nautch girls moving their limbs lazily but keep gyrating. I wonder what sustains these delicate maidens. This is the fun and entertainment part, other than which there is a parliament in session. Harmonic notes played by the bands, the sound of dancing feet, laughter at the table are all suffused with political frenzy. Every night followers of the Conservative and Liberal parties discuss the battles that take place in parliament with great interest. Such is the tizzy when London is in season. Then the tide ebbs out and London's full moon wanes. The fun and the frolic stop, and most of the people who remain in London are the infirm, or those who have a dire need to remain there, or those who simply don't want to go out. Leaving London becomes fashionable. I read in a book ("Sketches and Travels in London": Thackeray) that during this time some of those who remain in town close their front-side doors and windows and live quietly in the rooms farthest from the street to produce the impression that they have left London. Go to the South Kensington Gardens; there you won't find the laces, caps, feathers, silk, wool or the pink cheeks that light up the garden and dazzle your eyes like a rabble of butterflies. The gardens are green and the flowers are still in blossom but something is missing. The vehicles, the people and the motley assortment have cleared out of London.

London's season has just ended and we have also moved out to a semi-rural area known as Tunbridge Wells. I'm glad to breathe in the clean air after such a long time. Relentless smoke and dust from burnt rock coal and coal dust flying out of thousands of chimneys had settled on the very bones of London. I suppose it is possible to produce ink by washing one's hands off such pollutants in the street taps. And inhaling coal dust with air without a break must have made our brains highly combustible. Tunbridge Wells is famous for the mineral water from its natural fountain which is rich in iron. Travelers visit this place to drink this water. Upon hearing the word fountain we expected to see something very beautiful like mountains all around; trees and plants; warbling of egrets and swans; lakes full of lilies, water-lilies and white water-lilies in bloom; cuckoos cooing; gentle breeze; humming bumblebees; and finally absorption of the five arrows of the god of love in this scenic spot and returning home after a drink of nothing but pure fountain-water. Upon reaching the place we found a small amount of water slowly seeping through a little hole paved with stone in the middle of a village market and an elderly woman standing there with a glass tumbler. She was supplying fountain water to the visitors for a penny a tumbler and reading about yesterday's proceedings in parliament in a newspaper when she had nothing to do. There were sellers everywhere, not a sign of trees and there was a butcher's shop where hung the carcasses of various four-legged creatures and skinned ducks and swans seeing which I got so cross that my mind refused to believe that this fountain water could have any health-giving properties.

Tunbridge Wells is a very small town, a few steps and you are out in the open amongst foliage. The houses like those of London do not have pillars or porticos and the sloping roofs stand in staid straight-line formations. They lack grace. On the other hand the shops are well-decorated, neat and have glass windows giving ample scope of window-shopping. The butcher's shop has no glass panes. Legs of various four-legged animals and the different body parts of sheep, cows, pigs, and calves hang before your eyes in various fashions. The long necks of several birds including ducks hang upside down and a robust young man with a large belly stands in the doorway wearing a hemmed dress and carrying an enormous blade.

The sheep and cows of England are famous for their substantial meat and fine taste. If there were a cannibal tribe I would expect English butchers to sell at exorbitant rates in their village-markets. A lady tells me that she feels very happy when she sees a butcher's shop and is content in the knowledge that there is no shortage of food in the country, there is enough food to satisfy hunger and there is no possibility of famine. I feel sorry at the way the English deck their tables with meat. If you cut meat into small pieces before cooking, it is easy to ignore that you are actually eating an animal. But if the table is decked with large pieces of an animal where one can descry the face and limbs it produces the nauseating feeling that you're about to devour a carcass.

Wooden mannequin heads wearing various wigs of curly hair, and fake mustaches and beards are displayed in the barbers' shop windows and various branded and *infallible* anti-alopecia treatments are for sale. Women with long hair can visit these shops to have their hair washed and styled by male attendants. But the shops selling liquor are the most impressive ones. They are well-lit in the evenings, their buildings tend to be largish, the interiors are spacious and well-decorated and they are teeming with customers both inside and outside. The tailor's shops are also attractive. Fashionable clothes hang in their glazed shop windows which also have mannequins. They have a section for women's clothes and here are present by day and by night a number of window shoppers looking hungrily at the dresses. The fashionable women here who don't have the wherewithal to buy expensive dresses observe these dresses carefully in the shop windows and when they go back home they make similar dresses for themselves spending lesser than what the tailor would charge.

Near the house where we live is an open hilly place known as the 'Common' which means that the place is public property. The Common is open on all four sides, has a few large trees, is full of bushes and grass, is very green and due to the lack of variety among its plants has an empty look, a bit like a widow in a widow's traditional attire. The land is undulating and the bushes are thorny and I like the place very much. At places amongst the thorns and on the undulating earth, heaps of tiny bluebells blossom. At other places white daisies and yellow buttercups blossom in all their beauty. There are benches amongst the bushes and beneath the trees. This is where people come for a walk. There are so few people here and so much space that it is never crowded. Unlike the large gardens of London where there are confusing crowds of hatted people carrying umbrellas, here there are a few scattered couples sharing umbrellas sedentarily on far-away benches and some taking sequestered walks hand in hand. An enjoyable place in all. The summer isn't over yet. Here the mornings and evenings are exquisite. In full summer a little light is visible from two to three o'clock in the morning; four o'clock in the afternoon is when the sun shines most brilliantly and daylight is visible up to nine to ten at night. One day I woke up at five in the morning and went for a walk in the Common. I sat under a tree on the hill-top. In the distance the sleeping town looked like a picture; there was not a sign of fog. The empty streets, the high church towers, the houses all reddish with sunlight against the backdrop of the blue sky looked like a picture carved out of wood. But in reality, this town is not at all pretty. Each house here is just four walls with windows cut out of them with gabled roofs and ugly chimneys. As it became brighter, smoke poured out of hundreds of chimneys making the town appear hazy, people appeared on the streets and vehicles began plying. Shopkeepers started delivering bread, meat and curry to the householders from push-carts or horse-drawn carriages (here the shopkeepers go to the houses to deliver these goods). People started coming to the Common and I left for our rooms.

There is a place over here where I like to go for walks. The hilly road is uneven from the tracks left by the vehicles plying on it and is fenced on both sides with blackberry plants and and other dense climbers and bushes besides being surrounded by tall shady trees, grass and wild flowers like daisies. Workmen wearing coats and trousers as well as faces covered in dust and mud go up and down this road. Little children with plump cheeks can be seen playing outside their houses or on the road—I've never seen such healthy and plump children in any other country. There are small ponds next to the houses where domesticated ducks swim. Although the fields are hilly and uneven, the crop lands look even and clean. The grass is very fresh and verdant; since the sunlight is not harsh it doesn't look scorched as happens in our country and the fields look beautiful and comfort the eyes with their relatively cool green color. Some of the tall trees and white buildings can be seen in the distance looking rather small. Far past these green fields, there is a forest of giant pine trees which receives not much sunlight because of its density. It is very dark, very solemn and very quiet.

My Ninth Letter

It is summer and the sun looks beautiful. The clock strikes two. There is a sweet breeze much like our winter afternoons. My surroundings are warming in the afternoon sunlight and my spirits are high and I'm at the same time just a little distracted.

We are now living in Devonshire in a town known as Torquay which is by the seaside. The place is hilly. The sky is clear. There are neither any clouds, nor fog, nor darkness. Everywhere there is greenery, the birds are chirping and the flowers are blooming. When we were in Tunbridge Wells I would imagine that if the god of love were there he would have great difficulty fashioning his flower darts and would have to be content with a few wild flowers gathered from the woods and thorny bushes. But in Torquay, even if the love god were to build something like a Gatling gun which can fire a thousand darts in a minute and even if that gun were operational day and night there wouldn't be a shortage of flowers. Everywhere we go we seem to walk on flowers. Everyday we go roaming in the hills. We see the cattle and the sheep grazing, at some places the road is so steep that we have to walk with difficulty. At places the path is very narrow and passes through trees on either side which obstruct sunlight. Here and there broken steps of stone make climbing easier though. Creepers and bushes have sprung up in the middle of the road. Everywhere there is sweet sunshine. The air is quite warm and it reminds me of India. In comparison to London, this mild warmth is sufficient to make the animal life of this place lethargic. The horses are slow and so are the people, going about their lives lazily.

I like the seaside very much. When the tide comes in, the large rocks are nearly submerged with only their tips showing above the water, like isles. Right next to the sea are hills big and small and the waves have carved out caves in their lower regions. Some days, when the tide goes out, we sit inside these caves. Clear sea-water gathers in pits inside them, scattered here and there are sea-weeds, there is a healthy sea-smell and there are boulders and stones all over. Sometimes we try to move these boulders putting together our efforts; and we gather sea-shells and snails. Some of the rocks seem to be leaning on the sea. On some days we risk our lives to climb on top of them and watch the waves below. The wind moans, small sailboats sail away, it's bright and sunny and we lie on the rocks, umbrellas over our heads. Where else would I find such leisure? Some days I go to the hills and seek out a rocky and secluded place surrounded by bushes to read a book.

My Tenth Letter

Christmas passes and in no time it's New Year's Day. But there's hardly any shouting. I hadn't expected the New Year to dawn so silently. They say that in France the New Year is welcomed with much warmth. On New Year's Eve our neighbors had kept their windows open fearing that if they didn't the parting year wouldn't leave the house and the New Year would be forced to wait outside.

It has been many days since we have returned to London from Torquay. Here, I live with K...'s family. The household comprises of him, his wife, his four daughters, his two sons, three maidservants, me and Tebby the dog. Mr. K... is a doctor. His head and beard are almost completely white and he looks strong and handsome. Mrs. K... who is affectionate by nature and has a most affable countenance takes very good care of me. She censures me for not putting on plenty of woolens when it's cold. If she thinks that I haven't eaten adequately, she does not let me leave the table until she is well satisfied that I have. If perchance I happen to cough a couple of times in the day, she does not let me bathe, forces me to down a number of medications and before I retire she sees to it that some warm water is poured on my feet. Every morning the oldest Miss K... rises before everyone else. She comes down to inquire if breakfast has been prepared. She propels a few shovels of coal into the fireplace which makes the room quite warm. A little later you can hear the sound of heavy feet on the stairs as old man K... descends shivering and enters the dining room. After quickly warming his hands, feet, chest and back he sits at the breakfast table newspaper in hand. He kisses his daughter and wishes me good morning. He's a cheerful man. We engage in a bit of banter and he reads out sundry items from the newspaper. He finishes his first cup of coffee when his next two daughters come down and kiss him. He has an arrangement with them that if they rise before him then he will owe them 5 crowns each; however if he rises before them they will be fined a crown. The latter amount despite being so small they already owe him a few pounds. The creditor makes his claim every morning but the debtors laugh. K... says "This is very unfair". Sometimes he says to me, "Mr. T..., you tell us, is it proper to neglect one's debt of honor?" regarding me as sort of an impartial arbiter.

And the debt keeps mounting for want of payment. Mrs. K... enters next. We finish breakfast by about half past nine. Its been some time since Mr. K...'s older son has eaten breakfast and left for his office and K...'s younger son and youngest daughter have also had breakfast. I've all but forgotten Tebby the dog. He's been sitting near the fireplace for a while. Tebby is tiny and long-haired and his eyes and face are barely visible through the fur. He's an old dog and has gone blind in one eye. The K...'s dote on him and consequently he regards himself as no less than a prince. He doesn't like to rest anywhere other than in the drawing room and jumps up and sits on the best chair. If someone tries to share it with him, he gladly moves to the adjacent couch. Tebby receives his quota of three biscuits at breakfast. He sits with his biscuits in the dining room and waits for me to come and play with him sometimes taking them from his mouth, sometimes rolling them over to him. Earlier, if I rose late Tebby would bring his biscuits outside my bedroom and bark. But he's noticed that I get annoyed if he barks while I sleep. So he tries to push the door very quietly with his paws and sits outside until I open the door. And when I come out he wags his tail and jumps about merrily. Then he keeps glancing at his biscuits and towards me. Anyway, breakfast is finished by half past nine. After that Mrs. K... accompanied by the maids goes up and down the stairs from the third floor to the ground floor tidying things and supervising housework wearing gloves. She enters the kitchen to read the bills of the vegetable seller, the bread seller and the butcher and arranges for all the necessary payments. Sometimes she goes up to discuss housework with her husband. She assesses whether kitchen equipment and cooking ingredients are clean and in their right places. She investigates if the meat is of good quality and the weight is right. Sometimes she helps the cook. Thus she is occupied with domestic work from breakfast time to about half past one in the afternoon. Sometimes the oldest Miss. K... joins her. Everyday, her immediate younger sister cleans the drawing room with a cloth duster. And the next younger one sews the pillowcases, the socks and other clothes. On some days she sings being the musician of the household. The youngest son and daughter of the K...'s play with each other since school is closed for the holidays. After finishing lunch at half past one, we get back to our own businesses. This is when the visitors arrive. Perhaps Mrs. K... is sewing her husbands torn pair of socks in the drawing room, wearing a pair of spectacles. Her third-born daughter may be making a sweater for her nephew. The second-born daughter is making use of her leisure to read A Short History of the English People by Green sitting near the fireplace. The oldest Miss. K... has gone out to visit an acquaintance. Perhaps a couple of visitors arrive at three o'clock. The maid announces them in the drawing room as "Mr. and Mrs. A..." by which time they have entered. The housewife and her daughters greet the visitors keeping their socks, sweater and book aside. The conversation starts with agreement on the state of the weather. Mrs A... mentions, "Mr. X... got the measles at forty-three and had to take four days leave. He attended office yesterday and his colleagues are constantly ridiculing him over it." The others express their sympathies for Mr. X... Gradually they discuss everything they could about measles. Miss K... informs them that the third son of Mr. G... has contracted measles. From that the conversation turns to Mr. G...'s cousin Miss E..., who is in Australia and has just married Captain B... The A...'s leave after some more conversation. In the late afternoon we go out for a walk which is followed by dinner at half past six. We assemble in the drawing room after dinner, at seven o'clock. There's a fire burning and the room is warm. We take our places around the fireplace. On some days we sing.

By now I have learned many English songs. I sing while Miss K... from whom I've learned these songs plays the piano. But we also engage in reading in the evenings. On six days of the week we read six types of books and on some days up to almost twelve o'clock.

I've made good friends with the kids and they call me uncle Arthur. The youngest daughter of the K...'s, Ethel insists that I am solely **her** uncle Arthur. If her brother Tom claims me she protests. One day Tom wanted to tease Ethel and so he said, "My uncle Arthur". Ethel puffed up her lips and started crying clasping my neck. Tom is slightly overactive as kids tend to be. He's a good kid. He's plump and has a big head and a meditative countenance. Sometimes he asks me unusual questions. One day he asked me, "Uncle Arthur, what do rats do?" Uncle says, "The steal food from the kitchen". After pondering over the answer for a while he asks, "They steal? Hmm... why do they steal?" Uncle says, "Because they feel hungry". Not pleased with the answer Tom leaves the room. He's always been told that taking other people's belongings without asking for their permission is not right. If ever Ethel cries Tom tries to comfort her saying, "Oh, poor Ethel, don't you cry! Poor Ethel!" Ethel knows very well that she is a lady. She sits on the chair demurely and sometimes says to Tom reproachfully, "Don't disturb me." One day Tom fell down and was crying. I said to Tom, "Big boys don't cry". Ethel at once runs up to me and says, "Uncle Arthur, when I was a kid I fell down in the kitchen, but I didn't cry". When I was a kid!

Mr. N... is Dr. K...'s oldest son. Although he lives in the house he is rarely seen. He spends all day at office. Even when he is not at office he is rarely to be seen because he is courting Miss. E... to whom he has been betrothed. On Sundays, he goes to church twice with his fiancée. Sometimes he visits them in the late afternoon for a cuppa if he's free. He is invited to their place for supper Friday evenings. Thus he has very little time to spare. The couple is so happy and content with each other that they do not feel the need for any other form of companionship to spend their leisure. On Friday evenings even if there's a thunderstorm, Mr. N... carefully combs his hair after applying pomatum, brushes his coat clean and goes out with an umbrella. One day it was very cold and he had a terrible cough; I thought the poor man wouldn't venture out under such conditions. It was barely seven o'clock when he came down all dressed up and ready to go out.

I have grown very friendly with this family. The other day the second-born Miss. K... revealed to me that they were very frightened when they heard that an Indian was coming to live with them and she and Ethel had fled to a relation's house the day I arrived and had stayed there for nearly a week. They returned home only after they heard that my face and body were not thoroughly tattooed and my lips were not pierced for wearing ornaments. And the first two days after coming back they spoke to me without looking at my face. Perhaps they were afraid that I would turn out to be some strange-looking creature. And finally when they saw me—then?

I am living happily with the K...'s. The evenings are pleasant with song and music and reading. And Ethel doesn't want to let go of uncle Arthur for a moment.

CPSIA information can be obtained at www.ICGtesting.com
Printed in the USA
LVOW12s1613070814

398030LV00020B/1348/P